PENGUIN'S FAMILY

The Story of a Humboldt Penguin

SMITHSONIAN OCEANIC COLLECTION

For Eileen, Maureen, Bob, and Joe, with memories of runaway Winnebagos, waxed-paper slides, and Percy's Big Wheel—K.H.

For Amy, who fills my palette with bright colors, and a warm smile—D.J.S.

Book copyright © 2004 Trudy Corporation and the Smithsonian Institution, Washington, DC 20560.

Published by Soundprints, an imprint of Trudy Corporation, Norwalk, Connecticut

Book design: Shields & Partners, Westport, CT
Book layout: Bettina M. Wilhelm
Editor: Laura Gates Galvin

First Edition 2004
10 9 8 7 6 5 4
Printed in Indonesia

Acknowledgments:

Our very special thanks to Dr. Gary R. Graves of the Division of Vertebrate Zoology at the Smithsonian Institution's National Museum of Natural History for his curatorial review.

Soundprints would also like to thank Ellen Nanney and Katie Mann at the Smithsonian Institution's Office of Product Development and Licensing for their help in the creation of this book.

Library of Congress Cataloging-in-Publication Data is on file with the publisher and the Library of Congress.

PENGUIN'S FAMILY

The Story of a Humboldt Penguin

by Kathleen M. Hollenbeck   Illustrated by Daniel J. Stegos

Soundprints®
Where Children Discover...

I t is early morning on the west coast of Peru. Waves crash and withdraw as a warm autumn breeze blows across the rocky and barren shoreline.

A male penguin stands near the water's edge. He peers out over the sea and then waddles quickly to a small cave of rocks. Ducking inside, he sits gently on an egg resting there.

For more than a month, the penguin and his partner have cared for this egg. They have taken turns sitting on the egg to keep it warm. In the quiet of the cave, the penguin hears a faint tapping sound. He stands and looks at the egg. It is time for the chick inside to hatch.

Hours pass, and the tapping continues. By late morning, a small, pointed beak pokes a tiny hole in the eggshell. The shell is thick, and the baby penguin works hard to break free. Finally, the tiny bird emerges entirely from the broken shell. Wet and hungry, he peeps. Father Penguin moves close to warm Baby Penguin.

Baby Penguin's downy feathers dry quickly in the warmth of Father Penguin's body. Mother Penguin waddles into the cave. She feeds Baby Penguin mushed anchovies and other tiny fish she has brought from the sea. Then Mother Penguin and Father Penguin preen Baby Penguin, using their beaks to clean and arrange his soft, fine feathers.

For the next four weeks, Mother Penguin and Father Penguin take turns caring for Baby Penguin. While one swims and finds food, the other stays with Baby Penguin to protect him.

One morning, Baby Penguin waddles across the sand with Father Penguin. A hungry giant fulmar circles overhead. Without warning, the bird cries out loudly and dives from the sky, aiming straight for Baby Penguin! Father Penguin stands in the fulmar's way. The bird soars to the sky and gets ready to swoop down again.

Quickly, Father Penguin herds Baby Penguin into another cave of rocks. Baby Penguin huddles close to his father. The fulmar cannot reach them. Screeching, she flies away.

When he is almost ten weeks old, Baby Penguin learns to swim. He waddles to the water's edge. Warm water laps at his flippers. By instinct, Baby Penguin waddles deeper and dives in. Shaped like a torpedo, his body cuts smoothly through the water.

Away from shore, the water is much deeper and colder. Kept warm by his feathers, Baby Penguin swims on. Every few minutes, he pops his head above water for air.

One day, Baby Penguin sets off to swim alone. Father Penguin and Mother Penguin will not go with him this time. Baby Penguin will try to find food on his own.

Baby Penguin dives below the surface, hunting for small fish. He sees a school of fish overhead. The fish cannot see Baby Penguin because his black feathers blend in with the dark ocean water. Baby Penguin knows he must separate the fish. Then he can catch them one by one.

Baby Penguin steers with his feet and tail. He swims in circles just below the group of fish. Around and around he swims, faster and faster. The fish move closer and closer to one another. All at once, they scatter. Instantly, Baby Penguin swims up and catches many fish. He swallows them quickly, one at a time.

With a full stomach, Baby Penguin swims more slowly than usual. He grows tired and almost stops moving.

Baby Penguin turns to swim back to land. Suddenly, he senses danger in the water! A sea lion swims nearby. Baby Penguin's heart beats fast. He races toward the safety of the shore.

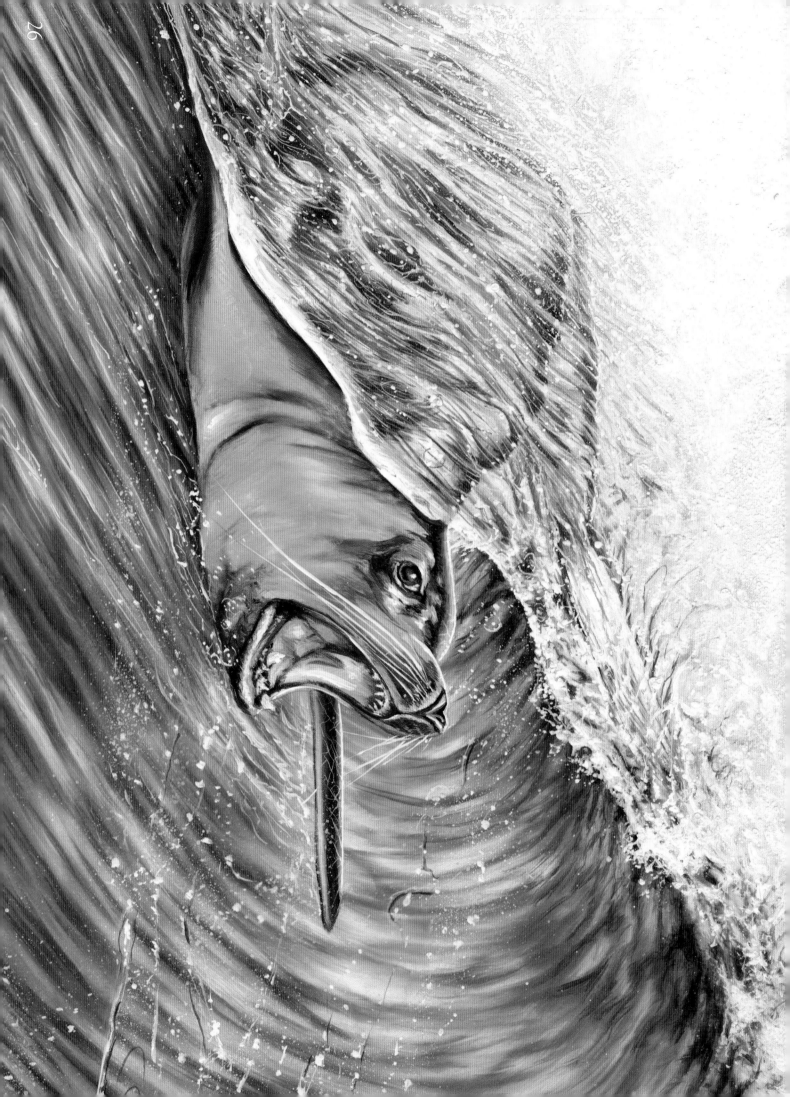

The hungry sea lion lunges at Baby Penguin. Just then, a mighty wave rises, tossing the sea lion aside and carrying Baby Penguin to safety on the sand.

Baby Penguin lies at the water's edge. Then he stands and calls out. His voice sounds low and squeaky, like the bray of a donkey. Mother Penguin and Father Penguin see Baby Penguin and hear his call. They know he is their own.

Together again, the family stands at the edge of the sea. Waves crash, birds cry and sunset paints the sky above their home along the Humboldt Current.

About the Humboldt Penguin

Humboldt penguins live along the Humboldt Current, a flow of cold water that runs north along the western coast of South America, off of Chile and Peru. Humboldt penguins are an endangered species of waterfowl. There are about 6,000 pairs worldwide.

Humboldt penguins nest in large colonies and mate for life. Each pair lays one to two eggs (usually two) a year. Humboldt penguins are known for speed and agility under water. Their bodies secrete oil that covers their feathers, insulating body warmth and repelling water.

Glossary

anchovy: A type of small fish.

torpedo: An underwater missile that moves swiftly and smoothly.

waddle: To take short steps and sway from side to side.

hatch: To break out of an eggshell.

downy: Soft and fluffy.

Points of Interest in this Book

pp. 14-15: giant fulmar.

pp. 20-21: school of fish.

pp. 24-25: sea lion.

pp. 6-7: tending an egg.

pp. 8-9: penguin hatching from its egg.

pp. 10-11: parents feed and preen newborn chick.